I0435627

Created by Village Tech Class of 2018
Design support provided by Todd Cowden

Village Tech Schools
1010 East Parkerville Road
Cedar Hill, TX 75104

Making Our Mark

Volume 1

Preface
by Todd Cowden

Identity. The individual characteristics by which a person or thing is recognized. From a personal standpoint, it defines who we are. For most people, their identity is created through experiences, choices and events that occur over a lifetime. But how well can you know your own identity with only a limited amount of years to pull from?

Ask yourself, "Who am I?"

Do you know your identity? Are you old fashioned or a tech head? Are you an all-star athlete or more of a book worm? Are you shy or outgoing? A leader or a follower? What if you could change your identity? What if you could craft it, design it? Imagine if you could mold it and shape it, choosing the person you wanted to be. Who would that be? Would it look any different than the person you are now?

Answering questions like these is what this project, and this book are all about. We asked one hundred ninth graders, just entering their freshman year in high school, to take a closer look at themselves and to design a personal logo around their identity. This book presents 26 of the most unique and interesting designs.

Some chose to become more aware of who they were at this moment in time. Others chose to look ahead to the future and where they saw themselves after they graduated high school.

The assignment put no limits on where the students envisioned themselves. Their dreams, not yet confined by the realities of "experience", were encouraged to be as large, or as small as they wanted to be.

Designing the logos took several steps. They learned to look not only at the positive, but also the negative space around their design. To be aware not only of what was there, but also what wasn't. To understand that "more" doesn't necessarily mean "better" and that sometimes it's the simplest of things can make the world of difference.

From thumbnails to tight pencils; concept to completed logo, it was an iterative, evolutionary process. It took time and patience. Mistakes were made. Lessons were learned, not the least of which was that every choice should have purpose. Every line, every letter, every decision had an effect on the overall design.

Some logos, for one reason or another, took longer to develop than others. Some students decided to start from scratch halfway through the project. But in time, they all eventually took shape. After six weeks everyone had a logo to present. Each one unique as the designers that created them.

When the students saved the version of the logo they were presenting I made a specific point not to include the word "final" as a part of the file name. These aren't the "final" versions. These logos, just like the students themselves, will be ever changing, developing, growing, and evolving. Some changes may be slight, others may be grand, changing almost every aspect of the original. But it's all part of the process…part of the design.

Yes, there were academic lessons and skills to be learned during this project. What is typography? How important are positive and negative space in a design? What is a thumbnail (other than that thing at the end of your thumb)? They learned about the Selection Tool, the Zoom Tool and the Pen Tool, but hopefully the tool they learned about the most…was themselves.

Introduction

by Isis Toldson
(9th grade student; Village Tech)

In this book you will find a story. A story of characters with dreams, and ideas, and personalities. You will find characters with memories, experiences, and stories that are unlike any others. Take a look and you will see the youth and the creativity of the next generation. Our dreams, our fears and our insane aspirations. You will find an NBA Allstar, an architect and a teacher. A designer, a writer, business owner and musician. You will find the Steve Jobs, Michael Jordan, and Oprah Winfrey of tomorrow. And still the star gazing dreamer of today. You will find people; people who have yet to realize their full potential.

In this book are the passions, hopes, fears, and very lives of 26 students who are tackling the question that has ruled the centuries, head on. A question that examines the very being of the asker and a question that it takes many their life and more to answer..."Who am I?" As high schoolers it is vital that we answer this question above all others because the world we live in has many ideas and opinions about who a typical teen should be, how a typical teen should act, and what a typical teen should dream, that we often blindly accept as reality. But one glance in this book and you will see that we are anything but typical, and over the past semester we have shed the suffocating skin of normal and opened the gates of impossible. We have embraced our outlandish dreams, unspoken fears, and unruly ideas, and unleashed an undying will to forge our own path in the world. We are the survivors of yesterday, leaders of today, and dreamers of tomorrow.

But do not be mistaken, what you will see is but a smudge mark on the canvases of our lives, this is only the first thousand words in the novel that is our story. A story whose every word is decided by the choices we make and who we have dreamed we could be. Now those dreams have been the centerpiece in discovering our identity. Our dreams are what make us strong, they are what make us brave, and what make us unstoppable. We will be chance takers, difference makers, and world changers. We will take this world by storm, and we will Make Our Mark.

Lois Foldson

Alex Balbuena

I am a 14 year old girl who loves books, movies and TV, in that order. I have loved to read since I was a little because of my mom who taught me how to read and introduced me to her favorite authors. I was always looking for the next thing to read and that lead me to finding the book blogging community. I have been reviewing books on my blog for over two years and I have attended countless events. I work for author, Romily Bernard and that job introduced me to the Public Relations/Marketing side of the literary world.

I aspire to get a degree in Public Relations and Marketing so that I can join a publishing company to work with books for the rest of my life. Books have been my love and my constant for so long that I knew that there was no way to make a personal logo without incorporating books into it. This logo is me as I live and breathe and I hope you see that.

ALEX

Tre Beacham

Hi, my name is Tre Beacham and my goal in life is to be successful in life. I am a leader, love to have fun, and am very creative. In my logo I put all three of these aspects into picture.

Using my leader like qualities I would like to own a restaurant or clothing store when entering my career. The sports car represents the expensive side of owning a business. Having fun is what I plan to do while living my life; and what is more fun the driving a sports car. The creative side of me is in the fount. The flame trailing the "B" just makes the car pop and thats what I want to do Make thing pop out at everyone. Making this logo was fun and gave me a chance to share my future with you and my school. You will see my name later.

My name is Jose Beltran I'm a student at Village Tech. I love to eat Mexican food and many other spicy foods. I'm very passionate about school and sports. I enjoy playing soccer, going out with friends, and love hanging out with an amazing girl. The way this ties into my logo is with risk to eat different food especially spicy food. In the logo I took a risk of making a "O" into a jalapeno and it came out great. The contrast with the graffiti letters and the jalapeno just flows so well. Thats what makes this a great piece.

Jose Beltran

Deciding to be a counselor at my age is crazy, especially a marriage counselor, mainly because I know nothing about marriage. My name is Kayman Carrington, I'm 15 years old and I go to Village Tech Schools. My family and friends tell me I'm a good listener and I'm good at giving advice. Even though I don't know much about love and marriage, I will listen.

Kayman Carrington

Kay**Ⅱ**an
marriage counselor

Brian Catlett

Hi, my name is Brian Catlett, but people call me "BJ", I am a student in 9th grade at Village Tech Schools. I am really interested in gaming and anime. I like all types of games but I'm specifically interested in medieval and fantasy roll playing games (RPGs). In the future I really want to do something that relates to gaming, such as becoming game designer.

I've always been interested in the process of making a video game and I think that it will be a really fun job to do. I tried to put some elements from medieval times into my logo. I thought the font was good because it looked like something out of an anime that I watch and the three triangles that replaced the A's in my name reminded me of one of my favorite games.

Brian Catlett

Jessica Conn

My fellow classmates already know what they want to be when they're older, where they want to go, and what they want to see. I however take a different route, I don't know what my future's going to be like I just take the things that come in my path step by step. Yes, I plan to go to college and get a degree. I want to leave my mark on the world I just haven't quite figured out what it is yet. This project made me think about what I really wanted to be when I get older, but I'm still growing and making decisions for what's best for me that's why I have the question mark above the "i". I chose the script font because I like reading stories, because they let me get to explore different lifestyles people live every day. So I like to think of myself of as not normal, but unique.

Jessica

Cade Croysdale

I am currently a 9th grader at Village Tech High School in Cedar Hill, Texas. All of my life I have gotten good grades. I have made the A&B Honor roll all the way through 8th grade. This year I hope to do better.

My inspiration for my logo design came from pure creativity. One thing that could possibly contribute is my Cherokee Indian background. That could explain the pointiness in my logo. It might resemble an arrow head, or maybe I just like pointy things.

Rachel Fender

My name is Rachel Fender. I am currently 14 and I'm a 9th grade student at Village Tech Schools. I have recently gotten into photography and realised that photography is something I want to do after college. Ever since I was a baby, I loved cameras.

When I was 2, I started taking pictures of whatever I could. They weren't very good pictures though. My mom would give me a camera every year and every time I went to camp. The pictures weren't the best but that was before I took a photography class at the Dallas Zoo a couple of summers ago. During that camp, I started taking my photography more seriously. I didn't take pictures just to take them, I took them because I thought that I could make the pictures seem like they were taken by a professional and not by me. I took my time and waited for the right moment.

I chose to make my logo a camera because photography has been a big part of my life before I could walk. Choosing the camera was not a difficult decision because it's something I really like to do. Photography is something that I'm happy doing and is something that I want to continue doing.

My name is Julien Gorena and I have many interests and hobbies, but making music is one of my favorite things to do. I created this logo intending to make it look like a musical equalizer, which is typically something you would imagine when you think of modern electronic music. The logo has no hidden meaning to it, but I plan to use the logo as a visual on my music videos if I ever upload my music to YouTube. Creating this logo was the first step to becoming the ideal producer I'd like to be.

Julien Gorena

My name is Morgan Gribble, I've been attending Village Tech since 8th grade. For the past two years I have been taking advanced art classes with Mr.Cahalan, it has opened my eyes to a whole new dynamic of art. Art has gone from my hobby to my career path, and I'm excited to see where it will take me!

My logo is painting my initial, which to me symbolizes the illustration of my future. There may be eraser marks and frustration along the way, but with failure comes progress, I'm ready to paint myself into history!

Morgan Gribble

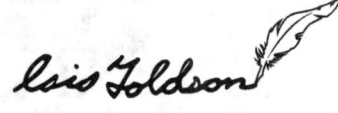

When I grow up I want to be a Pediatric Speech Therapist. The reason I chose my logo the way it is right now is to show a child by writing, spelling, and silently reading in their minds would give them the courage to verbalize what they're reading.

Maggie Hinojosa

Jonathan Hulbert

I am a person who can perform a lot of different skills. I can film, edit, act, and I love to make people laugh. I am very good with children and I work with them a couple times a month.

When I was making my logo, I focused on what I love to do and what I want to be. The two things I love most is filming emotions and making people laugh. As a result, I took a common associated item with film and I used it as my logo. This is how I came up with my logo idea.

Hello, my name is Grayson Ingram and the reason I decided to make my logo the way I did was because I want to be an architect. When I was very young, in kindergarten, we moved and I was old enough that I could go with my parents and look at some houses. Since then, I have always liked looking at houses and have wanted to design them. When I was about eight, I got a young architect kit for christmas in 2007 so I could design the floor plans of houses. Then in the summer of 2008, my family and I moved to a country in Africa called Tanzania and was away for about 5 years. I did not know what I wanted to be. In May of 2013, we came back in the United States and I am now going to a school called Village Tech in Texas, where we talk about our future and careers. There were other careers I considered, but I decided that I want to be an architect.

Grayson Ingram

Ever since I was a little girl I've had a love for animals. As I grew older, that love only got stronger. When I found out we were making a personal logo I just knew I had to incorporate my love for animals into it. When I graduate high school I plan to attend A&M University and major in Veterinary Medicine. Then someday start my own company in the animal business.

Apart from my love for animals I love reading, writing, watching movies, meeting new people and hanging out with my friends and family. I'm a freshman at Village Tech High School and am loving every minute of it!

Shannelle Jones

Shanelle J🐾nes

My name is Airiana Magdaleno, I am a freshman in high school, and this is my awesome logo! To tell you a little bit about myself, I am very athletic and I love to play select fastpitch softball. It is one of my passions and I've been playing since I was 9 years old. My dream is to become a professional softball player when I get older, and get paid for playing the sport I love. Also, I would want to have my own sports brand and sports products.

With that being said, I decided to incorporate my passion into my personal logo. As you can see, I have an A stacked on top of an M, which stands for the initials of my name. I also decided to put a black circle around the letters to make it look sporty and like a softball. And finally, the best part of the entire logo. I made the negative space of the A and the M look like the home plate on a softball field.

Airiana Magdaleno

Airiana Magdaleno

My name is Preston Myers. I am 15 years old, and a 9th grade student at Village Tech. During my spare time I like to longboard. It is one of my favorite hobbies and that is what I based my logo on. Longboards are like skateboards, but are longer and used for cruising, transportation, and downhill racing. I particularly like them because of the freedom I feel cruising down a hill, it gives me a scene of escape.

Preston Myers

Laina Scivally

The structure of my logo consists of my name and a butterfly. I chose to incorporate my name into the design because I think it represents me and my personality perfectly. I feel that my name is who I am. I decided to add the butterfly for a few different reasons. My main reason was because I believe it symbolizes my sisters and myself. My reasoning behind this is that we all three have an identical butterfly necklace so butterflies are basically a part of us. My oldest sister, Lauren believes they indicate hope, my older sister, Leah believes butterflies indicate faith, and I believe they indicate beauty.

When starting the process of creating my logo, my name wasn't even involved. I focused on the butterfly for the longest time. Once i realized my name is my logo, I thought adding it in would be absolutely perfect. My logo went through many iterations, until it finally hit version 6, the one you see here.

Laina

Hi my name is Treyvon but, some people call me Trey. I created this design because, music has been a big part of my life. I like to sing, make my own, or just make music on a DJ studio app. I hope to be in the gaming music industry or just make music for famous artists.

This design related to me because, I love music and it motivated me to do better on my work. I'd also like to become a great singer to, since I'm good at singing and I like to do it a lot. This is why, I chose to create this design.

Treyvon Simpkins

I'm Soleil Sipes, and this is is my logo. My logo, to me, connects to my innerself. I have a weird and unique personality, and I tried to make something that could relate to myself. My first name, "Soleil" actually means "Sun" in French . So the sun in my logo really represents what I stand for. The font was probably the hardest choice to make. There were so many choices to choose from. But the one I specifically choose meant the most to me because I write a certain way which is the closest to my writing style. Overall, my logo is unique, and defines me, and who I am.

Jada Stearn

Hi my name is Jada Stearn. I am 14 years old. My favorite hobbies are cheerleading, dancing, and shopping. When I grow up I want to become a Pediatrician and open up my own Pediatrics Doctors Office. Which explains the reasoning of my logo. I used the red cross to represent urgency in coming to my office and the medical field. I used the chalkboard font because Pediatrics is dealing with kids and most young kids use chalkboards. I want to become an Pediatrician because I love working with kids and I love the medical field so I figured putting the two together to pursue my career in.

JADA
Pedia✚rics

Isis Toldson

Since I was very small I've loved words. I learned to read at five like most kids, but unlike most kids I was at a twelfth grade reading level by fifth grade, but I had never considered writing. At the start of my sixth grade year I wrote a story about my fictional travels in the Sahara desert. After twenty embarrassing minutes my teacher stopped me and I lifted my eyes to find a class full of snickering peers. After class my teacher pulled me aside and told me that though long, my story had been entertaining and that I was a great writer. She said it as a random comment, but those simple words opened a world of wonder and possibilities.

Since then I have started a blog, written tons of poetry and short stories and I am working on my first novel. My logo describes me not only as a story writer, but as the unique writer of the incomplete novel of my life.

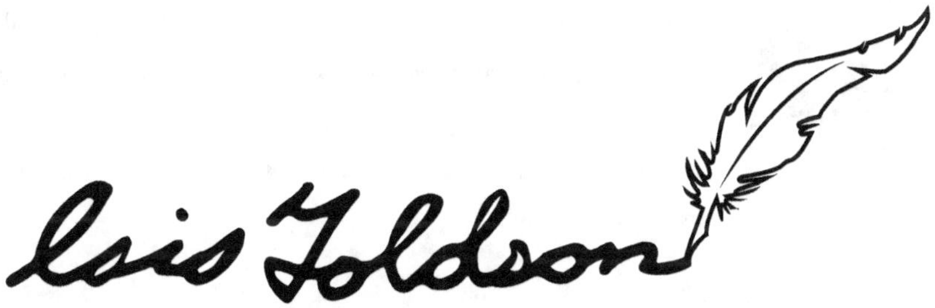
Isis Toldson

Danton Tunnell

My name is William Danton Tunnell. I am a freshman at Village Tech and percussion is a big part of life. I started percussion in the 7th grade and though Village Tech doesn't have a band, it still remains a big part of my life. This is reflected in my logo by the silhouette of a drumstick in the "T" and the single snare beat waveform in my last name. The reason I used my last name is because I have always played sports and all my coaches call me by my last name. GOOOOO SQUIDS!

My name is Nathan and my passion is video game design. I like playing video games like DayZ. I'm always thinking of ideas for this game I'm making, it's going to be a survival game. I have a YouTube channel and I try to post videos as much as possible. I also play the guitar and the piano. Video games have been a big part of my life, I have been playing since I was two.

My dream is to go to a university and find a job working as a game designer, but in the meantime, I work on my game.

Nathan Turner

GAMING

Corey Ward

My name is Corey, and I'm very honored to be apart of this book. My hobbies are singing, rapping, and basketball. The idea of my logo was basically a sports company that I just thought of. To me, sports is a lifestyle, and I was willing to express that through the illustration of the basketball between my first and last name. The font was to express my academic side of me.

As you should know, I'm serious about education and I tend to focus on that more than I do sports. My interests for my career are to either be an environmental engineer, or a professional wrestler.

Moving from academics, I also tend to focus on my extra curricular activities, such as my love for basketball. Basketball was the first sport I had ever played in my life and my love and I myself have become stronger and stronger in basketball. I actually want to be able to make some extra money by selling some athletic merchandise. So seeing that I'm an all around person, I love to take opportunities that I can to succeed in life. That logo explains it. It explains it all.

COREY WARD

My name is Morgan Weaver. I am energetic, very determined, nice and athletic. I like change and designing things, mainly rearranging rooms. My interests when I get older is to become an architect and my hobbies when I get older is interior decorating.

My initials are "M" and "W" and I added "design" in between to show that I plan on being an architect/interior designer. I am very creative and always wanting to draw, sketch or write things that come to mind. When I was designing my logo I wanted it to look sleek, neat and I wanted it to describe me as well as being simple. One of the difficult parts of creating my logo, was choosing a font that was what I had imagined, but I could only find one similar that I ended up liking more. I believe that my logo describes me very well and it came out better than I had imagined.

Morgan Weaver

Hello, my name is Darnell Williams and the one I wanted to do when I heard about the logo challenge I wanted to put a sign language "w" in my logo, but a lot of people thought the "w" was a three, so that's when I incorporated the world into my logo with "world" because I feel like the world symbolizes the many different languages in the world. Now I feel like the logo is completed and a whole lot better than my first iterration.

Darnell Williams

Your Name

You've taken a brief glimpse into the personalities and identities of 26 students. But we're all students in some shape and form. We're all learning to make our way through this world. All trying to make our mark.

What would your logo look like? What would it represent? What is it that you want to leave behind?

I, together with all the students in this book, and all of us at Village Tech, invite you to grab a pencil and use the adjacent page to create YOUR logo. It may start out rough, even sketchy, but give it some time to take shape. We encourage you to draw outside the lines. To not be bound by the limiations of your past. To be brave.

Be sure there's a purpose for every mark you make. And never, ever consider it "final".

Make Your Mark...

www.ingramcontent.com/pod-product-compliance
Lightning Source LLC
Chambersburg PA
CBHW071115280526
45787CB00003B/1058